The Art of Mme. Jehane Benoit:
fish

The Art of
Mme. Jehane Benoit:
fish

*A selection of the finest recipes from
Canada's best known cook and authority
on Canadian foods.*

By

Jehane Benoit

Greywood Publishing Limited

101 Duncan Mill Road • Don Mills, Canada

CONTENTS

INTRODUCTION

Have you ever tasted a delicately herbed baked lake trout, or a moist panbroiled salmon or halibut steak, a hearty fish mess, or a refreshing fish aspic? If you have, then you know how much you like fish. It does not take much effort to achieve any of this because to cook fish to perfection you have only to remember two things:

Firstly — Fish is highly perishable food therefore, the fresher the better. When purchased frozen, it is important to buy the best quality fish, and thaw it out just long enough to be able to separate the pieces.

Secondly — Fish, *at no time,* should be overcooked because it then becomes tough and dry. A good rule to apply is to cook any fish 10 minutes per inch of thickness (measure at its thickest part).

A half pound of dressed or cleaned fish or frozen or fresh fillets will serve one.

A third of a pound of fish steaks or sticks will serve one.

How to Buy Fresh Fish

Look for the following clues:
— There should be every little, if any, fishy odor.
— The flesh should spring back when it is pressed and be firmly attached to the bones.
— The eyes should be bright, transparent and somewhat protruding.
— The gills should be red and free from shine.
— A fresh fillet of fish should have a firm texture, a mild odor and no dried-out or brownish look around the edges.

What about Shellfish?

The rules for buying and cooking shellfish are the

same as for fish — the fresher the better, and never overcook.

Fresh Shrimps have a firm texture and a mild odor. The shells of uncooked shrimps range in color from grayish green to a light pink. When cooked their color changes to an all-over pinky red. The term " green shrimp" is a trade description for all uncooked shrimp.

A general rule is that one pound of shrimp will serve four. Of course, it depends on how big they are.

Fresh Lobster — A good live lobster moves its legs, however freely, and when picked up, it curls its tail under its body. If the hangs limp, the lobster is dead and should not be purchased.

The serving portions for lobsters depend on how big they are. One small lobster, of say 1 lb. in weight, will serve only one person. A larger lobster for two would suffice.

Scallops — In Canada, scallops are sold already cleaned, without their beautiful symmetrical shells. Although this makes the job of preparing them a lot easier, it also makes it a little less romantic.

Containing high levels of well balanced protein and very little fat, scallops are among our least expensive shellfish because most of the world's catch comes from the Atlantic coast. You can buy them frozen in 1 lb. packages or fresh by the pound. There are two kinds of scallops — "bay" and "sea". The sea scallop is larger and the meat is white. The bay scallop may vary in color from creamy white to pale pink.

Always take care not to overcook scallops as they'll be tough and stringy instead of tender and creamy. One pound will serve 6 small portions.

FROZEN FISH

Nutritionists and doctors think so highly of fish as a health food that we are apt to find it on every diet, whatever the reason behind the diet. This in itself seems to be a good enough reason for eating fish regularly.

Shellfish and other seafood are a luxury, so are fancy fresh salmon and other whole fresh fish. However, we have little excuse to forego serving fish on the grounds that it is too expensive or that we do not have good fresh fish available because we have a true convenience food in frozen fish. It is easily available; can always be kept in readiness in our own freezer; and takes only minutes to cook. The only thing needed for success is to have good recipes and be aware of how cook it properly in order to bring out its naturally delicious flavor. Another interesting point is that most fish recipes are interchangeable, with very little variation in their cooking times.

Handling and storing frozen fish is easy; keep it frozen until ready to use. Once it is thawed, do not refreeze it. If you freeze your own fish, remember that poor paper or improper packaging will cause gradual loss of moisture and the fish will shrink and dry out.

I have a rule when I buy frozen fish, to keep it only 4 to 6 weeks in my own freezer as I have no knowledge of what has happened to the fish before I bought it. If you use your refrigerator freezer compartment, keep it no longer than 2 weeks.

The question that often puzzles is whether frozen fish should be cooked immediately when it is taken out of the freezer. It is definitely better thawed out before being cooked and here is how to do it. Defrost the fish by placing it in the refrigerator until pliable enough to be handled. One pound of fillet will take 18 hours to reach this stage. This is the very best method.

The next method is to cover the box with cold water, then let cold water run over it. The length of the thawing process in this case depends on the size and shape of the fish — usually 30 to 50 minutes.

In an emergency, place the steaks or fillets directly under cold running water and they will thaw out in 30 minutes.

The worst way to thaw frozen fish is by leaving it out of the refrigerator on the kitchen counter. Although it is always the risk that the thinner parts of the fish will thaw more quickly than the thicker parts and spoilage can set in.

One very interesting fact to know is that frozen fillets or steaks do not have to be completely thawed. When set in the refrigerator for an hour or two, it is usually possible, in most cases, to cut them up or separate the pieces.

11

PREPARING FISH

I know a fisherman who will eat his fish cooked only one way — over red coals patiently built up with dry maple wood and peach stones, dried from the summer before. When the fire is right, he rubs a double wire broiling rack with olive oil, places his freshly caught cleaned fish on it, and sets it over the red embers to broil 10 minutes on each side, basting frequently with a mixture of melted butter and fresh lime juice (he would never go fishing without a few limes). When the last 3 minutes of cooking come around, he grinds black pepper on the fish, turns the grill and repeats the process. Then he slides it onto hot plates which contain hot lime juice. Finally he brushes the fish with melted butter and sprinkles it with salt. Never have I eaten finer broiled fish! But I do know a few other excellent methods — and some important points to keep in mind when preparing fish.

Always keep the fish as dry and as cool as possible. To clean, scrape off the scales — there are good scrapers available at sport shops or hardware stores. Then slit the belly from vent to gills with a good sharp, stubby knife and pull out all gill matter and innards. Some dark matter will remain under a membrane beneath the backbone — cut it open with the point of the knife and scrape it all away (if the fish is small, simply push your thumbnail along the cavity). Wash the fish as little as possible, wipe it dry, then remove the head and tail, if you wish.

If you want to fillet the fish, don't clean it first as this makes it more difficult. With a sharp, lightweight knife, cut around the top of the head to separate cartilage behind the gills from the flesh; be careful not to cut into the body cavity. Then make a long cut from head to tail on one side of the backbone and close to the top fins. At the tail end, cut through to the rib cage and slide the knife under the flesh to separate the back of the fillet from the bones.

Continue working forward, cutting away the rest of the fillet from the ribs but leaving as little flesh as possible on the carcass. You should be able to slice off the fillet quickly in one piece without touching the cavity. Proceed in the same way on the other side, then throw away the carcass.

To remove the skin from the fillets, lay them on a flat surface, skin side down. Begin at the tail end and work your knife between the skin and flesh. Hold the loose end of the skin and slice forward with the blade flat against the inside of the skin, or pull away quickly. On certain fish, the skin pulls right off.

And, when packing fish, do not let it get too wet. An

almost sure way to ruin fish is to pack it in ice with the result that the ice melts and wets it badly.

The best method is to clean the fish, as previously outlined, then pack each one in a separate plastic bag, excluding as much air as possible. The bags can be set over ice in a portable refrigerator.

I often roll the fish in corn meal or farina after cleaning, as this absorbs more moisture.

COOKING FISH

One of the important talents of a good cook is the ability to tell when a food is cooked just to the right point. A recipe can help to a degree but a natural sense about food, coupled with intelligence, will tell you the exact moment. When it comes to fish, the best and only advice is to not overcook. If the heat you use is too high or the cooking too long, the fish will be dry and tough and the house will smell of fish.

With fish, contrary to other food, the purpose of the cooking process is not to tenderize it as it is already tender, but to develop the flavor and coagulate the flakes so that they will hold together.

If you take notice attentively, you will see that the flesh of the fish loses its transparency in a short time when it is exposed to heat; the very moment that it turns opaque, you know it is almost done and only seconds are required to finish the cooking. Long additional cooking will only toughen and dry the meat of the fish.

Learning to check the translucent or transparent quality of the flesh of cooked fish is the best method to test for doneness. Remember every time you cook fish that it is cooked to develop the flavor — not to make it tender, as it is already tender.

Fat Fish Versus Lean Fish

I am often asked what the difference is between fat fish and lean fish.

The difference, as far as the one who cooks is concerned, is that the oil that lean fish contain is concentrated in the liner and the oil that fat fish contain is distributed all over the body. Therefore, the fat fish needs much less fat to cook it. This is important to know as too much fat used in cooking fish will make it more greasy and drier.

The best fat to use is oil, or half oil and half butter.

A gourmet's trick I learned many years ago in Italy is to keep 6 to 8 black olives and a few cloves of garlic in a pint bottle of corn oil; this gives it a beautiful flavor to fry fish with.

General Information

— In any recipe you can substitute other fish for the ones that are specified.
— Any large fish may be baked, with or without stuffing, or steamed.
— Any fish steak may be broiled, baked, or poached.
— Any fillet may be sautéed, poached, panfried, or baked in a sauce.
— Citrus fruit such as lemon, lime, grapefruit and orange make marvellous endings for fish dinners.

The Chinese Method of Broiling Fish

Water is the secret of this method. High heat is used as the fish is protected by the humidity of the water.
— Place the fillets on an oiled rack set in a skallow boiling pan.
— Sprinkle (do not roll), the fillets generously with fine breadcrumbs and dot with butter.
— Pour ¼ inch of hot water in the pan.
— Preheat broiler to 550°F. or for 15 minutes. This is important.
— Set the broiler pan 3 to 4 inches from the source of heat.
— Broil *exactly* 5 minutes, unless you are broiling very thin fillets which may take only 3 minutes.

Fish Baked in Polyester Film (LOOK)

I like this method especialty when cooking halibut or other types of frozen fish steaks.
— Thaw and dry the fish steaks with absorbent paper.
— Rub one side of each steak with a bit of soft butter.
— Place each piece on a square of film large enough to wrap properly.
— On each steak place a thin slice of onion, broken into rings (when possible, use Italian sweet red onion), and a slice of unpeeled lemon.
— Melt 2 tablespoons butter with the juice of ½ a lemon, ¼ teaspoon of marjoram or thyme, salt and pepper to taste.
— Spoon a small spoonful on each fillet. Fold film carefully.
— Place in a shallow baking pan. Add ¼ cup hot water.

— Bake in a preheated 400°F. oven, for exactly 20 minutes.
— Unwrap and serve.

Pan Fried Frozen Fillets

Pan frying frozen fillets has several disadvantages. They are more difficult to cook this way; the pan is usually hard to clean; and if the moisture is not well taken care of, the fat will spatter.

This is the way to proceed:

— Completely thaw the fish in the refrigerator. Open box and wrap each fillet in a piece of absorbent paper. Refrigerate 1 hour.
— Sprinkle both sides of fillets with salt, pepper and paprika.
— Roll in fine dry breadcrumbs or fine cracker crumbs or flour. Let the fish stand for 10 minutes, the coating will dry the top of the fish.
— Fry the fish in ⅛ inch of just hot salad oil, or half oil and half butter. Fry over medium low heat, turning the fish *only once*. Use a spatula to turn the fish.
— The cooking takes 10 minutes per inch of thickness. Measure at the thickest part of the fish before cooking. If only ½ inch thick, 5 minutes are required etc.
— Turn the fillets when 2 minutes of the cooking time are left.
— *Warning:* If a second batch of fish has to be cooked, wipe the hot pan clean with absorbent paper and add fresh fat; otherwise the second batch will have burnt spots and the fine taste of the fish will be lost.

Stuffed Frozen Fillets

Those who like stuffed fish often feel it is not possible to do it with the frozen fillets. On the contrary, there is an Irish way to do it, which is very tasty. Try it with low cost frozen cod fillets.

— Thaw 2 lbs. cod fillets, or other of your choice, in the refrigerator until they are pliable.

— Prepare a bread stuffing in the following way: Cook in ¼ cup bacon fat or butter, 1 cup diced celery and 1 large onion, minced, just long enough to soften the onion. Add 4 cups soft bread cubes, ½ teaspoon salt, ½ teaspoon sage or poultry seasoning, 3 tablespoons milk, 1 egg, beaten. Mix thoroughly.

— Spread this stuffing in a shallow well greased (with bacon fat) or buttered baking pan. I like to use a Corning dish that I can bring from the oven to the table. Lay the thawed out cod fillets on top of the stuffing in a single layer.

— Melt 2 tablespoons butter with ½ teaspoon each of paprika or curry and salt. Drizzle over the fish.

— Bake in a preheated 350°F. oven 30 to 35 minutes. Serve as is or with a tomato sauce or an egg sauce. Serves 6.

FISH FUMET

Fumet, used in haute cuisine as part of the liquid in fish sauces, or to poach fillets, or small fish, is almost a must for the French touch. A very concentrated *court bouillon,* it always contains fish bones, heads, or tails, or all three. It will keep a few weeks refrigerated or three months frozen.

1½ - 2 lbs. fish trimmings
(bones, heads, tails, fins)
2 cups water
1 bay leaf
1 onion, sliced
2 cups any white wine
1 carrot, brushed and sliced
2 celery stalks, in 1 inch pieces
2 tbsp. chopped parsley
¼ tsp. each salt and pepper

Bring all the ingredients to a boil in a heavy saucepan, cover and simmer 1 hour, or until liquid is reduced by half. Pour into a sieve lined with cheesecloth, letting it drip through untouched for about 30 minutes. Makes about 3 cups.

COD

I think of cod as the old faithful. White other fish come and go according to season, cod, from the Grand Banks of Newfoundland, is always with us.

A lean, flaky fish, it's available in fillets, steaks, sticks, and comes fresh frozen, salted, pickled, flaked, smoked or shredded. Even cod tongues are available — a unique delicacy.

While in Canada it is the most neglected of all fish, a forgotten delight, the Europeans make interesting and tasty dishes with cod. Why do we drag behind? I am convinced it is because we truly do not know how to cook it.

BOILED COD

This recipe, made with fresh cod, shows how it can be served as an attractive party dish.

3 - 5 lbs. fresh cod, in one piece
1 tbsp. coarse salt
8 cups cold water

26

10 peppercorn or ½ tsp. pepper
cut peel of 1 lemon

Rinse cod and brush all over with salt. Cover and let stand 1 hour in refrigerator, then place in the cold water with peppercorns and lemon peel.

Heat until water is warm, then simmer, uncovered, for 10 minutes per inch of thickness of fish, or until it flakes. When ready, remove fish from water with a perforated ladle. Set on a hot platter. Top with a few sprigs of parsley and serve with bowls of the following garnishes.

Potatoes boiled in their jackets; melted butter with grated lemon peel to taste; finely chopped raw onions mixed with parsley; chopped hard-boiled eggs; and grated raw apples (stir in a little lemon juice so they won't darken).

Let guests take their choice of garnishes. Serves 6 - 8.

BAKED STUFFED COD

We so rarely think of baking a fresh 4 to 5 lb. cod, yet it is so good. The result will surprise you.

4 to 5 lbs. fresh cod in one piece
1 cup cracker crumbs
¼ tsp. pepper
1 tsp. each salt and parsley
1 small onion, minced
1 tbsp. capers or 1 tsp. sweet pickles, chopped
¼ cup finely chopped bacon
½ cup light or rich cream
5 thin slices of salt pork

27

Wash the cod under running cold water. Wipe dry with a paper towel.

Combine the remaining ingredients except the slices of salt pork. Stuff the cod with this mixture and tie. Place the fish on a baking sheet lined with polyester or foil paper. Preheat oven to 350°F. Dredge the fish with a little flour and pour a cup of cold water in the pan. Place the salt pork on the fish and bake 60 to 80 minutes, basting frequently. Do not let the fish get dry. Remove carefully to a hot platter. To taste, add to pan juices ½ teaspoon curry powder and 2 tablespoons chutney or sweet relish and 1 tablespoon butter. Heat, stirring all the time. Serve as gravy. Serves 6.

COD FILLETS GRAPEFRUIT

Fillets or steaks can be used, fresh or frozen this is unusual and most pleasant.

6 cod fillets or steaks
seasoned flour
2 tbsp. butter
3 tbsp. salad oil
¼ cup cream
1 large grapefruit
2 hard cooked eggs
chopped parsley

Roll the fillets or steaks in the seasoned flour. Heat the butter and salad oil in a large cast iron frying pan. Brown the fillets over medium heat, about 10 to 12 minutes, turning only once.

In a small saucepan heat 1 tablespoon butter, add the

cream and the juice of ½ the grapefruit. Chop the eggs and add. Heat together, but do not boil. Salt and pepper to taste.

Set the fish on a hot platter and pour the sauce over. Sprinkle with parsley.

Cut the other half of the grapefruit in two and slice thinly. Place around the fish. Serves 6.

BAKED NORWEGIAN COD FILLETS

This is one of my favorite ways to serve cod fillets — crisp and brown with a nice, creamy sauce.

> 2 lbs. cod fillets, fresh or frozen
> 2 tbsp. salt
> 1 tbsp. vinegar
> 1 tbsp. melter butter
> 1 egg white, lightly beaten
> ½ cup fine breadcrumbs
> ½ tsp. turmeric
> 3 tbsp. grated cheese
> ½ cup dairy sour cream

If fillets are frozen, thaw just enough to separate. Rub each fillet with salt and vinegar mixed together, then set on a platter and refrigerate 1 hour.

Dry fish with absorbent paper, brush with melted butter and dip into egg white. Mix breadcrumbs, turmeric, cheese, and roll fillets in mixture. Place side by side in a well oiled baking dish and bake uncovered at 350°F. for 15 - 20 minutes. After the first 10 minutes, add 2 tbsp. water.

When done, remove fillets to a hot platter. Add sour

cream to pan juices and simmer, stirring until well blended and hot but do not boil. Taste for seasoning and pour sauce around fish or serve separately. Serves 6 - 8.

SALT COD PAYS BASQUE

The Spaniards, Portuguese and Basques are masters at cooking cod. This simple recipe is a good example.

2 lbs. salt cod
2 cups milk
flour
¼ cup salad oil
2 onions, thinly sliced
1 garlic clove, sliced
3 peeled tomatoes, sliced
½ tsp. sugar
pinch of cayenne
salt and pepper, to taste
2 slices bread, diced

Cut cod into pieces and soak for 12 hours in water, changing water 3 or 4 times during the first few hours.

Cover with fresh cold water and add 2 cups milk. Slowly bring to a boil, drain, and remove all the bones you find. Let cool, then roll each piece in flour.

Heat oil in a cast iron frying pan and brown fish on both sides over medium heat, turning only once. As pieces are browned, place in shallow ovenware casserole.

Add more oil to the pan if necessary and fry onions and garlic. When browned, add tomatoes, sugar, cayenne, salt and pepper and simmer 2 minutes. Pour over cod and bake at 375°F. for 10 minutes.

In the meantime, brown bread cubes in a little bit of oil in the same frying pan. Cool, crush and, when ready to serve, pour over fish. Serves 6.

COD LOAF

A precious recipe, when any cooked cod is on hand. Equally good served hot or cold.

2 to 2½ cups cooked flaked cod
2 green onions, chopped
¼ cup finely diced celery
½ cup chopped celery leaves
1 cup toasted breadcrumbs
¼ tsp. marjoram
salt and pepper to taste
2 eggs, separated
½ cup cream or milk
½ cup melted butter or margarine

Preheat oven to 375°F. Butter generously a 2 quart mold.

Combine the fish with onions, celery, celery leaves, breadcrumbs, herbs and seasonings.

Beat the egg yolks with the cream or milk and add the melted butter. Pour over the cod mixture. Mix well. Taste for seasoning. Beat the egg whites until stiff and fold them in.

Pour into prepared pan and bake 40 minutes or until the loaf has set. Unmold on a hot platter. Serve as is or with a tomato sauce. To serve cold, cool and refrigerate in its pan. Serves 6.

HALIBUT

Halibut ranks as Canada's seventh most important fish food and it is found on both coasts of the Dominion. However, the most important catch is made in the waters off Northern British Columbia and in the Gulf of Alaska. British Columbia is close to the world's greatest halibut fishing grounds, an area that yields more than 60 percent of the world's annual halibut catch. The Atlantic halibut is caught off the coast of Nova Scotia and in the Gulf of St. Lawrence as well as on the offshore banks but Nova Scotia contribuates the major portion of the Atlantic's halibut landings. These short notes on our Canadian halibut industry should encourage everyone to taste and surely cook more often this delicately flavored fish. We can find it fresh and frozen most of the year in our stores but April is the month *par excellence* to eat fresh halibut.

I recall my amusement the day I saw a live halibut for the first time — with its two large eyes, the upper one slightly behind the lower one. So flat in shape, dark brown

34

on the upper side with lighter irregular blotches, the lower side white, and such small and smooth scales. It gave me the feeling that it was a fish which refused to be ignored. Another interesting fact is that halibut do not spawn until they are 10 to 12 years old. At that age, a large female halibut of 140 pounds may have as many as 2,700,000 eggs. The young ones enter life in an upright position with eyes on each side of the head and both sides of the body the same color. Gradually as the baby halibut becomes a young halibut the left eye migrates or twists over towards the right side of the head and the body starts to change color.

Too often we forget that biologically speaking "fish is meat." It is more than a meat substitute, it is a meat alternate which means it contains proteins, vitamins, minerals and other nutrients of the proteins of the same high quality as meat. Another plus is that fish is easily digested and so fast to cook. So, let us cook in as many ways as possible one of our national foods, the halibut.

BROILED HALIBUT STEAK AMBASSADEUR

Broiled or barbecued is perhaps the best way to serve fresh halibut in order to have the impact of its full nice flavor and it is so easy to do.

1 small halibut steak per serving
salt, pepper, paprika
1 tablespoon butter
1 tbsp. salad oil
1 tbsp. lemon or lime juice

1 tsp. brandy
fresh dill or chives, minced

Wrap the steak in absorbent paper. Refrigerate 1 hour. Unwrap, place on a well oiled shallow baking pan. Sprinkle to taste with salt, pepper and paprika.

Melt the butter with the salad oil, lemon or lime juice. When boiling hot, pour over the steak. Broil 4 inches from the source of heat 4 minutes on each side, turning only once. Serve as soon as ready, place on a warm platter and pour on top the brandy mixed with dill or chives.

To barbecue, proceed in the same manner doubling the butter, oil and lemon mixture, using half to baste the steak at least twice on each side; turn only once. Cooking period is the same.

HALIBUT BEAUFORT

Breaded baked halibut prepared from this classic of the French cuisine is never dry or overcooked. The garnish is most colorful.

6 small halibut steaks
½ cup butter
1 cup fine breadcrumbs
1 tsp. curry powder
1 egg
2 tbsp. water
1 green pepper
1 medium-sized onion
1 tbsp. salad oil
1 tsp. sugar
salt and pepper

Melt the butter in an elegant shallow baking dish. Mix the curry with the breadcrumbs. Beat the egg with the water. Dip each steak into the egg mixture, then roll lightly in the curried breadcrumbs. Dip quickly in the melted butter on both sides. Set one next to the other. Bake 15 minutes in a preheated 400°F. oven.

In the meantime, clean the green pepper and slice paper-thin into round rings. Slice onion thinly and break into rings. Heat the salad oil, put in the green pepper and onion rings, sprinkle with the sugar, stir gently over medium heat for 4 to 5 minutes, just to heat through and soften lightly. Salt and pepper to taste. Pour over cooked halibut and serve. Serves 6.

HALIBUT OYSTER BROIL

I enjoyed this exciting dish at the table of a sheep farmer in Vancouver Island, sitting in his beautiful garden surrounded by flowering trees, on an April day filled with sunshine. It has become one of my favorite halibut recipes.

1½ to 2 lbs. halibut steak
juice of 1 lemon
¼ tsp. paprika
salt, pepper to taste
½ pint oysters
1 tbsp. butter
2 tbsp. flour
2 tbsp. butter
1 cup milk
⅓ cup mayonnaise

2 tbsp. lemon juice
¼ cup relish
3 tbsp. chopped olives
2 green onions, minced
1 tsp. strong prepared mustard

Place the halibut on an oiled shallow baking dish, when possible one that can be brought from oven to table. Mix the lemon juice with the paprika and use to brush the fish on both sides. Salt and pepper to taste. Place in a broiler 3 inches away from the source of heat and broil 6 minutes. Turn and top with the oysters, evenly distributed over the halibut. Dot with the tablespoons of butter and broil until the edges of the oysters ruffle. Top with the following hot tartar sauce and serve.

Make a white sauce with the flour, the 2 tablespoons of butter and the milk. When smooth and creamy, add the rest of the ingredients and season to taste. Simmer together (do not boil) for a few seconds. The sauce can also be served separately and the top of the cooked halibut sprinkled with minced chives or parsley. Serves 6.

BAKED HALIBUT CREOLE

If you are not too keen on fish, this is the way to start appreciating it. Halibut has a mild flavor; the topping is somewhat like Spanish sauce over eggs; and the work so easy. Serve it with boiled buttered and parslied rice.

2 thin slices of salt pork or 4 slices of bacon
1 medium-sized onion, thinly sliced
1 halibut steak, about 1 inch thick

salt and pepper
¼ tsp. curry powder
1 cup canned tomatoes, drained
1 tsp. sugar
¼ cup sliced black olives (optional)
⅓ cup breadcrumbs
2 tbsp. melted butter

Place half the salt pork or the bacon, cut into 1-inch pieces, in the bottom of a baking dish. Place half the onion on top, then the halibut steak. Sprinkle the fish with the salt, pepper and curry powder. Drain the tomatoes, measure and mix with the sugar, olives and remaining onions. Pour over the fish. Top with the remaining salt pork or bacon. Melt the butter, mix with the breadcrumbs. Sprinkle over the whole. Bake in a 375°F. oven for 30 minutes. Serves 4.

HALIBUT FLEURETTE

The sauce in this case makes the dish. Sauce Fleurette is very popular in the South of France and should be better known because it is delicate and very tasty. A perfect way to serve halibut for a buffet dinner.

6 individual halibut steaks
2 tbsp. butter
½ cup water
½ cup white wine*
salt to taste
2 tbsp. melted butter
2 tbsp. flour

½ cup milk
1 cup fish stock (from the cooked halibut)
salt and pepper to taste
⅛ tsp. nutmeg or mace
2 tbsp. minced parsley or chives
1 tbsp. lemon juice
1 tsp. butter

Place the halibut steaks, one next to the other, in a shallow baking dish. Pour on top the water and white wine. Sprinkle lightly with salt. Cover the dish with a sheet of buttered paper (not foil paper). Place in a preheated 475°F. oven for 15 minutes. Remove the fish from the pan with a perforated spoon. Set on a hot dish, while making the sauce. Pass the fish stock through a seive. Measure 1 cup and set aside.

To make the sauce, melt the 2 tablespoons of butter in a saucepan, add the flour and the milk and fish stock, stir until creamy and smooth. Salt and pepper to taste, add the nutmeg or mace and the minced parsley or chives, stir together over low heat until well blended. Remove from heat, add the lemon juice and the teaspoon of butter. Stir until the butter is melted. Pour over the fish and serve. The last bit of butter added to the sauce is called, in French cuisine, buttering the sauce, and it does just that but it must never be put back over heat. Serves 6.

* The wine can be replaced by the juice of 1 lemon and enough apple cider to come up to the half cup mark.

BROWN BUTTER HALIBUT

A "take-off" from the classic Eggs au Beurre Noir. Served with buttered long grain rice and green peas flavored with fresh mint, it is a meal to please the most demanding.

4 halibut steaks
½ cup milk
½ tsp. salt
¼ tsp. freshly ground pepper
grated rind of ½ a lemon
¼ cup flour
1 tbsp. butter
2 tbsp. salad oil

Brown butter:

1 tbsp. cider vinegar
2 to 3 tbsp. butter
1 tbsp. finely minced parsley

Mix the milk with the salt, pepper and grated lemon rind. Measure the flour onto a meat plate. Roll each halibut steak in the seasoned milk, then roll in the flour. Heat the 1 tablespoon butter with the salad oil in a frying pan. When hot, put in the halibut steak and fry over medium heat 4 minutes per side, turning only once. Set on a hot platter.

To make the brown butter: add the vinegar first to the fat left in the frying pan; set over high heat; add the butter; stir quickly without a stop until the butter has a nutty brown color; pour over the halibut and serve.

To make Halibut Amandine, proceed in the same way, adding ¼ cup of blanched almonds, cut into long slivers, at the same time the butter is added. The almonds will brown as fast as the butter. Serves 4.

HALIBUT STEAK SAUTE

Salmon steak prepared this way is as good as halibut. An excellent basic recipe for fish steak.

halibut steak 1 to 1½" thick
lemon juice
flour seasoned with paprika, salt and thyme
1 tbsp. butter
2 tbsp. salad oil
grated rind of ½ lemon
1 tbsp. parsley, minced

Dip the halibut steak in lemon juice, then in flour seasoned with paprika, salt and thyme.

Melt the butter in a heavy metal frying pan. Add the salad oil. When hot, add the prepared fish. A 1½ to 2 lb. piece of halibut will take 8 to 10 minutes to cook.

To serve, mix together the lemon rind and parsley and sprinkle over the fish. Serves 4.

FINNAN HADDIE

I never knew what true Finnan Haddie was until I ate *Cullen Skink* in Scotland at a dear friend's family farm which was surrounded by big black fir trees, through which came the fierce winds and clamors of the North Sea. Then I learned that Finnan or Findon Haddocks were so named from a small village near Aberdeen, where they had the best of them. In the old days, they were smoked, dried over seaweeds, and sprinkled with salt water during the smoking period. Now they use peat smoke. On this side of the world, Finnan Haddie has a golden color, but through the commercial processing it has lost the nutty flavor and rich texture of true Finnan Haddie. Yet, properly prepared and cooked, our cellophane wrapped type still has a "bit of a touch of the old Aberdeen."

To come back to my first experience with "Finnan", I remember when the "good cook", as my friend called her, asked us whether we wished to eat Findon, Aberdeen, Arbroath or Auch Nuttie type of Finnan Haddie.

I was quite at a loss to answer. I settled for the Findon type which was the right thing to do as I have never forgotten it.

Our Scottish ancestors brought this delicacy to our shores. As a child I remember my mother serving "Scots Fish" — which was, of course, Finnan Haddie. As it is one of our colonial dishes, we should all try to learn how to cook it to perfection and it is possible. I have, during the War, eaten a "Poached Finnan" equal to my remembrance of the Scottish type, in Halifax, at the delightful Sword and Anchor. I never understood why this place disappeared. It had such wonderful old charm that it could have been one of our Colonial monuments.

Basically, Finnan Haddocks can be grilled, steamed, poached or made into a loaf. They have an affinity to butter, milk and potatoes. They are a budget item and seem to please even those who care little for fish. Badly cooked, they are dry and unpleasant.

ST. ANDREW'S GRILLED FINNAN

In Scotland the St. Andrew's type is heavily smoked and served mostly grilled. Topped with a poached egg, it is a treat I often enjoy.

1 lb. Finnan Haddie, cut in to 4 portions
1 cup hot milk
3 tbsp. unsalted butter or margarine
4 poached eggs (optional)
¼ cup minced parsley

Place the fish in a dish; pour the hot, but not boiling, milk on top. Cover and let stand 4 hours. This will tenderize the fish and prevent the drying effect from direct heat during the grilling period. Remove from milk, wipe as dry as possible with absorbent paper.

Cream the butter and spread on one side of fish, reserving 1 tablespoon. Place buttered side up on a grill and set 4 inches away from source of heat. Grill 4 minutes, turn and grill 2 minutes. Poach the eggs while the fish is cooking. To serve, place the fish on a hot plate, top each piece with a poached egg, and sprinkle the whole with the parsley. Add 3 to 4 tablespoons of the soaking milk to the melted butter in the bottom of the grill pan. Heat over direct heat and pour over the fish. Serves 4.

FINNAN FARMHOUSE SCRAMBLE

Serve on a cold night with hot buttermilk biscuits. In Scotland, it is a good "Crofter" specialty.

1 lb. Finnan Haddie
1 cup milk
2 to 3 tbsp. butter
salt and cayenne to taste
¼ cup chopped parsley
4 eggs
the juice of ½ a lemon

Pour the milk over the fish in a shallow pan. Simmer, covered, over low heat for 10 minutes or until the fish is tender. Remove from milk and flake.

Melt the butter in frying pan, add the flaked fish, salt, cayenne and parsley. Stir over low heat for 2 to 3 minutes.

Beat the eggs in a bowl and pour over the fish mixture. Cook slowly to make scrambled eggs. Do not overcook. When ready, remove from heat, pour the lemon juice on top and serve.

The remaining milk could be thickened with a tablespoon of cornstarch, mixed with a couple tablespoons cold water, to make a parsley sauce to serve with the scramble. Salt and pepper to taste and add as much minced parsley as you would like to have. This should be done before scrambling the eggs. The fish can be kept warm while you make the sauce. Serves 4.

FINNAN SAVORY PUDDING

All that is needed to make an elegant, tasty meal with this light soufflé type pudding is a green salad.

1 lb. Finnan Haddie
2 slices bacon
1 tbsp. butter
2 cups mashed potatoes
salt, pepper to taste
juice of ½ a lemon
1 small onion, minced
½ tsp. celery salt
3 tbsp. minced parsley
¼ tsp. savory
3 tbsp. butter, melted
3 eggs

Place the fish in a shallow pan. Top with the bacon and just enough water to cover the bottom of the pan.

Cover and steam 10 minutes over medium heat. Remove fish to a plate. Rub with the tablespoon of butter. Cool. This is the basic way to steam Finnan Haddie.

Flake the cooled fish and stir into the mashed potatoes. Add the salt, pepper, lemon juice, onion, celery salt, parsley and savory. Beat until the whole is thoroughly mixed. Melt the butter and add to the mixture.

Separate the eggs and beat the yolks until light and stir into the fish mixture. Beat the egg whites until stiff, fold gently into the fish.

Butter a casserole or soufflé dish, pour in the mixture. Bake in a 350°F. oven for 30 to 40 minutes or until golden brown and puffed up. Serves 6.

WREXHAN FINNAN SPAGHETTI

English farmhouse native cooking, the recipe was given to me by Mrs. Cowking, who had inherited it from her grandmother and mother. That was many years ago, in 1945 to be exact. I still enjoy making it.

1 lb. Finnan Haddie
¼ tsp. savory
8 ounces spaghetti or elbow macaroni
4 slices bacon
1 large onion, thinly sliced
3 tbsp. butter
3 tbsp. flour
2 cups milk
salt, pepper to taste
½ to ¾ cup grated cheese

⅛ tsp. nutmeg
1 cup diced bread

Place the fish in a saucepan with 2 cups boiling water and the savory. Cover and simmer over low heat for 10 minutes. Remove to a plate, cool and flake.

Boil the spaghetti or elbow macaroni according to directions given on the package. Drain and place in a bowl.

Dice and fry the bacon, add the onion and fry until light brown. Add to the spaghetti with the flaked fish.

Make a white sauce with the butter, flour and milk. When smooth and creamy, salt and pepper to taste, remove from heat, and add the cheese and nutmeg. Place the fish mixture in a casserole dish. Pour the cheese sauce over all. Top with the diced bread that can be rolled, to taste, in a few tablespoons of bacon fat or melted butter. Bake in a 350°F. oven for 25 to 30 minutes. Serve hot. Serves 6.

FINNAN SAVORY

The way the Old Country use the leftover Finnan Haddie: as a creamy breakfast dish or on toast as an after dinner savory. Use cayenne to flavor a savory, chutney or curry powder for breakfast.

1 tbsp. butter
cayenne to taste or ½ tsp. curry powder
1 to 1½ cups flaked cooked Finnan Haddie
2 tbsp. cream

1 tsp. capers
chopped fresh parsley

Melt the butter, add the cayenne or curry powder. Stir until butter is light brown, add the flaked fish, cream and capers. Simmer over low heat, until the fish has absorbed most of the cream. Salt to taste.

For breakfast, serve in a hot dish, sprinkle with parsley. As a savory, serve on squares of hot buttered toast, topped with parsley. Serves 4.

SALMON

POACHED SALMON HOLLANDAISE

Halibut is as good as salmon served in this manner.
2 lbs. salmon in one piece
⅓ cup melted butter
⅓ cup dry vermouth or lemon juice
salt and pepper to taste
foil

Place the salmon on a large piece of foil. Set on a dripping pan. Bend the foil around the salmon without covering. Pour the melted butter and the vermouth or lemon juice over the salmon. Salt and pepper to taste.

Bake in 350°F. oven, 40 minutes. When cooked remove from oven. Close foil to completely cover the fish. Cool, then refrigerate 12 hours. The juice turns into a delicious jelly that is served with the fish. Serve with Blender Mustard Hollandaise. Serves 4.

BLENDER MUSTARD HOLLANDAISE

Use your blender for a minute and you'll have perfect hollandaise. If you don't have a blender, follow your favorite recipe and add the teaspoon of mustard when sauce is cooked.

4 egg yolks
2 tbsp. fresh lemon juice
1 cup (½ lb.) butter
4 tsp. very hot water
½ tsp. salt
few drops of Tabasco
1 tsp. Dijon style mustard

Combine the egg yolks and lemon juice in blender, cover and blend 10 seconds at high speed. Melt butter until it bubbles. Gradually add hot water to yolks while blending at medium speed, then add hot butter in a slow, steady stream.

Turn off blender, add remaining ingredients, cover and blend at high speed 30 seconds. Pour into a serving dish, cover and keep at room temperature. It's best to make this early on the day it's needed rather than the day before. Yield: 2 cups.

POACHED SALMON A LA FRANÇAISE

The French use salmon steak for this colorful and tasty dish. It is then as easy to make for 2 as for 10. It is served with the classic *sauce verte*.

4 - 6 salmon steaks
1 tbsp. salad oil
juice of 1 lemon
peel of ½ lemon, grated
6 peppercorns, crushed with back of spoon
1 tbsp. salt
1 small onion, quartered
3 - 6 sprigs parsley

Spread the oil in a frying pan (I like to use the teflon coated type), or in a flat baking dish. Place the salmon slices next to one another, but not overlapping. Add the lemon juice and peel, peppercorns, salt, onion and enough hot water to just cover the fish. Cover and poach on top of the stove (if in frying pan) over low heat for 10 - 20 minutes; or in a 325°F. oven (in baking dish) for the same length of time, or until the salmon flakes.

Allow the fish to cool in the liquid. Drain well and remove the skin. Arrange on a serving platter, then completely cover the fish with the following sauce. Serve with a cucumber salad. Serves 4 - 6.

SAUCE VERTE

If you have a blender, this sauce will be ready in minutes. If not, the ingredients will have to be chopped very finely.

½ cup green onion tops or chives
½ cup green pepper
¼ cup parsley
½ cup spinach, uncooked
2 tbsp. lemon juice
1 cup mayonnaise

Chop the vegetables coarsely and place in blender with lemon juice. Cover and blend until it turns into a sort of mush with small bits of this and that in it. Add to the mayonnaise and blend.

Without the blender, chop the ingredients very finely and blend into the mayonnaise, crushing them to give as much color as possible to the sauce. Makes 1½ cups.

ENGLISH POACHED SALMON

A most attractive way of serving salmon for a buffet supper or garden party.

4 - 6 lbs. fresh salmon
2 cups milk
2 cups water
1 tbsp. salt
2 bay leaves
¼ cup parsley, coarsely chopped
½ tsp. basil
¼ tsp. dill seeds
1 cup mayonnaise
2 hard boiled eggs
1 peeled lemon, thinly sliced
2 carrots, finely shredded

Wrap salmon in cheesecloth. Bring the milk, water, salt, bay leaves, parsley, basil and dill seeds to a fast boil. Boil 5 minutes. Add salmon and simmer, covered, over medium low heat for 20 to 35 minutes.

Let fish cool in its water. Then remove from water, but do not unwrap. Cover and refrigerate until ready to serve.

To serve, unwrap, remove the skin, place on a silver platter, garnish by spreading mayonnaise and making a long line of overlapping lemon slices on top. Grate the eggs and sprinkle over the whole fish. Place the finely shredded carrots all around to form a red crown. Serves 6 - 8.

POACHED SALMON WITH DILL DUMPLINGS

Country fare, most delicious and a meal in itself.

2½ - 3 lbs. fresh salmon
1 tbsp. salt
½ unpeeled lemon, thinly sliced
1 bay leaf

Whenever possible, choose salmon from the tail end as it is more attractive when served.

Put the fish in lukewarm water to cover, add salt, lemon and bay leaf. Cover and simmer 40 to 45 minutes. Slowly cooked, the salmon will be tender and remain juicy. Uncover and cool in the broth. Remove skin and leave in broth until ready to serve. When prepared ahead of time, reheat in the broth by just bringing to the boil.

While the fish is cooking make a tomato sauce in the following manner. Fry 1 finely chopped onion in 2 tablespoons butter. Add 2 cups tomato juice, ½ teaspoon sugar, ½ teaspoon dill seed or 1 tablespoon fresh dill, 1 tablespoon chopped parsley, salt and pepper to taste. Simmer 5 minutes. Set aside.

Make Dill Dumplings in the following manner. Sift 1 cup flour with ¾ teaspoon salt and 2 teaspoons baking powder; cut in 1 teaspoon butter, 1 teaspoon lard or 2 teaspoons butter; add ¼ cup chopped fresh dill and bind with ½ cup of milk or a little more if needed, use just enough milk so pieces of dough may be nipped off and rolled into small balls. Roll in flour and chill 15 minutes to 2 hours in the refrigerator. This will make 9 to 12 dumplings, depending on their size. Bring the sauce to a boil, drop in the dumplings, cover tightly and simmer 12 minutes. Place around the salmon on a hot platter, top with the remaining sauce and sprinkle with chopped dill or parsley. Serves 6 - 7.

HOT SALMON MOUSSE

This is a very popular entrée before a light or cold main course. If you like, serve it with a cold cucumber sauce flavored with dill; the contrast of hot and cold is very pleasant.

16-oz. can sockeye salmon or
1½ lbs. fresh poached salmon
¾ tsp. salt
¼ tsp. pepper
juice and grated peel of ½ a lemon
1 tsp. Worcestershire sauce
2 green onions, very finely chopped
3 egg whites
1 cup light or heavy cream

Remove the skin from the fish, crush bones with a fork and pass salmon through a food mill, large mesh sieve or food chopper. Add seasonings, green onions and stir until thoroughly mixed.

Add unbeaten egg whites, one at a time, beating hard after each addition, then gradually mix in cream. Pour into a well oiled 1½ quart fish mold, or any mold of your choice. Place in a pan of water and bake in a 375°F. oven, 40 - 50 minutes.

Let mold rest 5 minutes, then unmold onto a hot platter. Serves 4.

If you want to make the cucumber sauce, shred 1 unpeeled medium cucumber, place in a sieve and let drain. When ready to serve, whip ½ cup of heavy cream, add cucumber, ½ tsp. of salt, a pinch of cayenne and juice of ½ a lemon. Serve cold in a sauceboat.

SCOTTISH MOLDED SALMON

An attractive way to use those leftover bits and pieces of a good poached or baked salmon, or start with a thick slice of poached salmon.

2 - 3 cups cooked salmon
1 envelope unflavored gelatin
¼ cup cold water
1 cup mayonnaise
2 tsp. prepared mustard
1 tsp. curry powder
capers
lemon wedges
shredded lettuce

Remove skin and bones from salmon, pack pieces into an oiled mold of your choice. Cover and refrigerate for a few hours. Sprinkle gelatin over the cold water to soften for 5 minutes. Set over a pan of hot water to melt. Mix together the mayonnaise, prepared mustard and curry powder; add the gelatin slowly while beating constantly. Refrigerate for 10 minutes.

Unmold the fish onto a service platter. Spread generously with the jellied mayonnaise. If any is left, spread it around the unmolded fish. Decorate the top with dots of capers. Place lemon wedges around, standing up against it. Surround with a thick layer of shredded lettuce. Refrigerate until ready to serve. Serves 6.

SWEDISH SALMON AND VEGETABLE SALAD

This is a good way to use leftover salmon, but canned salmon will substitute very nicely. On picnics, I take along all the ingredients, measured in assorted jars, and a 1 lb. can of salmon. Then I have only to mix them.

1½ cups cooked or canned salmon
2 peeled tomatoes, chopped
1 peeled cucumber, diced
1 cup cooked or canned green peas
2 tsp. lemon juice
1 tsp. sugar
1 tsp. salt
½ tsp. pepper
½ cup mayonnaise
lots of chopped parsley

Flake the salmon and mix it lightly with the tomatoes, cucumber and peas. Beat together the lemon juice, sugar, salt, pepper and mayonnaise. Add to the fish mixture and blend lightly.

Pile in a neat mound in a serving dish or bowl and cover thickly with parsley. Cover and refrigerate until needed. Serves 4 - 6.

QUEBEC POTATO PIE

Use leftover cooked salmon or canned salmon; both are nice. It makes a family meal served with coleslaw.

pastry for a 2 crust pie
5 - 6 potatoes
1 small onion, chopped fine
½ tsp. savory
salt and pepper to taste
½ - 1 lb. cooked salmon or 1 (6 or 12-oz.) can salmon
1 can creamed corn or corn kernels or
2 large onions, minced and fried

Line a pie plate with a crust of your choice.

Peel and cook the potatoes, mash, and add onion, savory, salt and pepper. Blend together and spread over the pie crust. Cover with the flaked salmon and then add the corn or mince 2 onions, fry and place over the salmon. Cover with the second crust.

Bake in a 400°F. oven 30 to 35 minutes, or until golden brown. Serve hot. Also very good served at room temperature. Serves 6.

SCALLOPED SALMON CASSEROLE

A flexible casserole because you can use an equal amount of cooked flaked cod or halibut instead of salmon, or you can try the higher priced but delicious crab

60

or lobster. This won't freeze, but can be refrigerated a couple of days, then reheated at 375°F.

16-oz. can pink or red salmon
milk
1 tbsp. instant minced onion or 2 green onions, diced
3 - 4 sprigs parsley, chopped
1 tsp. salt
¼ tsp. each thyme and pepper
1½ cups crushed shredded wheat cereal
butter or margarine

Drain liquid from salmon into a 1-cup measure, fill cup with milk and set aside. (If using cod or halibut, simply measure 1 cup of milk). Flake salmon, crushing the small bones. Add cup of liquid and remaining ingredients except cereal and butter. Mix well.

Sprinkle bottom of a 9 inch casserole with a layer of crushed wheat, dot with half the butter and pour salmon mixture on top. Sprinkle with remaining crumbs and dot with rest of butter. Bake in a 375°F. oven 25 minutes. Serves 6.

SALMON LOAF

Although not overly fond of fish loaf, I find this one light and tasty. It's good value because these ingredients make 2 large or 4 medium loaves. If you wish to halve the recipe, 4 cups of leftover cooked salmon may be used.

4 1-lb. cans red or pink salmon
4 slightly beaten eggs

1 tsp. turmeric
1 tsp. curry powder
1½ cups milk
2 cups crushed potato chips
4 tbsp. melted butter
¼ cup chopped fresh dill or ½ cup chopped fresh parsley
salt and pepper, to taste

Open the cans of salmon and, without draining the liquid, empty their contents into a large bowl. Remove the salmon skin, crush the bones with a fork, and flake the fish. (Red salmon is richer in flavor, but it's also more expensive than the pink, so I sometimes use 2 cans of each.)

Add the remaining ingredients and blend thoroughly. Place in 2 buttered 4-cup loaf pans, or 4, 2-cup loaf pans and cover with foil. Label, date and freeze. Makes 10 - 12 servings and stores for 2 - 2½ months.

To use: Defrost loaf at room temperature for about 1 hour, uncover and bake at 400°F. for 30 - 40 minutes. This is very nice served with an egg or celery sauce.

SOLE AND OTHER FILLETS

SOLE AMANDINE

One of the best known delights of the French cuisine, this is easy enough to make and versatile. (Halibut can be used instead of sole.) What is most important is to cook it only when ready to serve, with no advance preparation.

4 - 6 fillets of sole
5 tbsp. butter (unsalted, if possible)
1 tbsp. salad oil
⅓ cup slivered blanched almonds
juice of ½ a lemon
chopped parsley
lemon wedges

If using frozen fillets, thaw just enough to separate. Salt and pepper fillets, then heat butter in a heavy metal frying pan, add oil and cook until it has a nutty color.

Place as much fish in the pan as comfortably fits, and cook over medium heat, 3 minutes per side, turning once only. When done, transfer to a warm platter and set aside in a warm place. In the remaining butter, cook almonds until golden, stirring constantly, and pour over fish. Swirl lemon juice in the pan, pour over, then garnish with parsley and lemon wedges. Serves 4 - 6.

FILLETS OF SOLE CHABLIS

Chablis is a white wine from Burgundy, and it's perfect with sole. You can, however, use any dry white wine or a dry cider in this.

> 4 equal size fillets of sole
> 3 tbsp. butter
> 2 green onions, minced
> 1 cup Chablis
> 2 tbsp. flour
> 1 cup light cream
> juice of ½ a lemon

Stretch each fillet on absorbent paper and pat it dry. Melt 1 tablespoon of the butter in an ovenproof dish or frying pan, add green onions and sauté lightly. Remove from pan. Put fillets in the pan, one next to the other, sprinkle green onions on top. Pour the wine over and place uncovered in a 350°F. oven. Poach 15 minutes, then remove fillets to a hot platter with a slotted spatula. Place pan over direct heat and boil until wine is reduced by half, then lower heat to medium.

Meanwhile, blend the remaining butter and the flour into a ball. Add cream and lemon juice, but do not mix. Pour into reduced wine and stir with a spoon or beat

with a wire whisk until sauce is smooth and creamy.
Salt and pepper to taste and pour boiling hot over the
fish. Serves 4.

SOLE BERCY

This one tops my list of favorites for its simplicity.
It is the different possible combinations of ingredients
that give each variation of this dish a special finish.

2 French shallots or 4 green onions
¼ cup chopped fresh parsley or 1 tbsp. dried parsley
¼ cup white wine
¼ cup fish fumet or clam juice
1 - 2 lbs. fillets of sole
juice of ½ a lemon
3 tbsp. butter, salted or unsalted
finely chopped parsley

Sprinkle the shallots or onions and the parsley over
the bottom of a generously buttered, shallow baking dish,
then add wine and fumet or clam juice. Lightly salt and
pepper both sides of the fillets, and set over ingredients
in baking dish (they can be placed side by side, slightly
overlapping, or folded in three.) Sprinkle with lemon
juice and dot with butter.

Cook uncovered in a 350°F. oven 20 minutes, basting
twice with pan liquid, then broil a few seconds to brown
here and there. This is good surrounded by small boiled
potatoes. Garnish all with parsley and serve immediately.
Serves 6.

FISH IN FOIL

This method is best with filleted fish and the results will be good done on an oven grill, barbecue, or campfire.

fish fillet of your choice
for every 2 lbs. of fillet:
¼ cup white wine or water
juice of ½ a lemon
1 tsp. butter
¼ tsp. salt

Bring all ingredients, except fish, to a boil and let cool. Place fillets in a bowl, pour cooled mixture over, cover and let stand 1 hour. Wrap each fillet in heavy duty foil, retaining as much dressing as possible on each. Use a double thickness of foil if fillets are to be cooked directly on coals.

Place wrapped packages on oven grill, barbecue or on the coals and cook 12 - 18 minutes, depending on the thickness of the fillets. A 1 inch thick fillet takes 12 minutes, so cook others either more or less. Serve piping hot in individual packages.

FISH FILLETS BONNE FEMME

Fresh or frozen fillets of a fish of your choice can be prepared with this French cuisine classic.

2½ - 3 lbs. fillets
2 tsp. salt
¼ tsp. pepper

3 tbsp. butter
2 cloves garlic, minced
1 medium-sized onion, cut in thin rings
3 green onions, chopped
½ to 1 lb. fresh mushrooms, cut in four
1 cup dry white wine
½ cup rich cream

Wipe the fish, sprinkle with salt and pepper. Melt the butter in a large frying pan, add the garlic, onion, green onions and half the mushrooms, sauté over high heat until soft, but not browned.

Place the fillets over this mixture.

Place the remaining mushrooms on the fillets and pour the wine over all. Cover the pan and simmer over low heat until fish is tender, usually 6 to 8 minutes. Gently remove the fish to a hot platter. Take most of the mushrooms out with a perforated spoon and arrange on top and around the fish.

Whip the cream until fairly thick, then quickly fold the pan juice in it and pour over the fish. Serve at once. Serves 6.

POACHED GREEN FISH

Green is for the generous coating of parsley that must cover the cooked fillets. This is a classic of the German cuisine.

2 lbs. fresh or frozen fish fillets
5 cups boiling water
3 onions, thinly sliced

1 bay leaf
1 tbsp. fresh dill or 1 tsp. dill seeds
¼ tsp. each thyme and peppercorns
2 tbsp. butter
1 tbsp. flour
2 tbsp. fine, dry breacrumbs
½ cup finely chopped parsley

Cut each fresh or partially thawed fillet into individual portions. Place in a saucepan and pour boiling water over. Add onions, bay leaf, dill, thyme, peppercorns and 1 tbsp. of the butter. Bring to a boil, take pan off heat and cover — the heat of the water will cook the fish.

Melt remaining butter, mix in flour, add breadcrumbs and 1 cup of the fish stock. Simmer, stirring constantly, until creamy and smooth. Pour into a warm serving platter, place cooked fish on top and completely cover with the parsley. Serves 6. (The leftover fish stock can be frozen and used as the liquid in any fish sauce.)

TROUT AND BASS

MOUNTAIN RAINBOW TROUT

Or small lake trout or any fresh or frozen trout, available individually or in a 10-ounce package.

Further enhance the flavor of the crisp corn-coated trout with a squeeze of fresh lemon juice.

⅔ cup yellow cornmeal
¼ cup all purpose flour
2 tsp. salt
½ tsp. paprika
6 large fresh or frozen trout

Combine cornmeal, flour, salt and paprika; coat fish. In a frying pan, heat a little cooking oil over hot coals for about 10 minutes. Cook fish 'til lightly browned on one side, about 4 minutes; turn and brown other side, about 4 minutes. Cook 'til fish flakes easily when tested with a fork. (Take care not to overcook.) Serves 6.

POACHED TROUT, CLAM DRESSING

Many women have fresh trout brought home by their husbands — this is a good way to prepare the extra ones because they'll keep in the refrigerator for 3 - 5 days. Frozen fillets of sole sliced in ½-inch blocks can replace the trout.

2 tbsp. salad oil
1 - 2 lbs. fresh trout, whole or filleted
1 tsp. salt
chopped parsley or dill, to taste
juice of 1 lemon
5-oz. can baby clams
¼ tsp. marjoram or thyme
12 - 15 stuffed olives, slices

Pour the oil into a baking dish and, without overlapping the pieces, place the whole or filleted trout in it. Sprinkle with the salt, parsley or dill, and lemon juice.

Drain the clams and pour their juice over the fish. Sprinkle with the marjoram or thyme and cover the dish with a lid or foil. Poach at 375°F. for about 25 minutes.

Cool, then drain the juice carefully without disturbing the fish. Refrigerate the fish, broth and clams separately.

When ready to serve, mix together the reserved clams and sliced olives. Add the broth, stir and taste for seasoning. Pour the dressing over the fish and serve with a bowl of radishes and tomato slices. Serves 4 - 5.

TROUT MEUNIERE

Another French specialty, this one is very popular with men as lunch time dish. Though extra delightful with fresh trout, it is also very good prepared with frozen speckled trout (all kinds are good, of course, but not so readily available.)

2 lbs. fresh or frozen trout
4 tbsp. flour
½ tsp. salt
¼ tsp. pepper
⅛ tsp. thyme
½ tsp. paprika
1 tbsp. salad oil
4 tbsp. butter
juice of ½ lemon
1 tbsp. finely chopped parsley

Thaw the frozen trout or wash the fresh type thoroughly. Using scissors, trim fins close to the skin, accentuating the tail by cutting it into a V-shape to make two distinct points. Roll fish in a mixture of flour and seasonings.

Heat oil and 2 tbsp. of the butter in a heavy frying pan, and cook fish over medium heat about 6 minutes per side, turning once only, until golden brown. Place on a hot serving dish and keep warm. Wipe frying pan with paper towels, then add remaining butter and cook over medium heat until nutty brown. Add lemon juice, salt and pepper to taste. Pour over fish while still foaming, sprinkle parsley on top, and serve immediately. Serves 4.

POTTED TROUT

Since all our supermarkets sell these frivolous, delicious little trout, frozen two to a package, this isn't as exotic as it reads. But it's just right for two gourmands, and is prepared ahead of time.

2 small trout, fresh or frozen
¼ cup all purpose flour
1 tsp. butter
2 tbsp. salad oil
pinch of curry powder
salt and pepper, to taste
butter

If using frozen fish, thaw according to package directions. Roll each trout in the flour and melt butter over high heat in a large cast iron frying pan. Add oil to the pan and, when very hot, add curry. Stir with a fork, then add the trout.

Lower heat to medium and fry trout 5 minutes on each side, turning once only. Season, set on a dish and let cool a bit. Then carefully lift flesh off bones and place in a small dish, either in one piece, or cut in four.

Melt some butter and pour over fillets until they're well covered. (Using a small dish is more economical since only the top needs to be covered with butter.) Cover and refrigerate, it will keep 8 - 10 days.

Serve the trout cold with a basket of toast and a bottle of chutney. Spread the trout butter on the toast and top with a bit of chutney. Serves 2.

STUFFED STRIPED BASS

Bass is a seawater autumn fish. Any other 3 lb. fish can replace the bass. My favorite wine to cook and serve with this is a Muscadet.

2 - 3 lb. bass
4 green onions, chopped
2 medium-sized, chopped
⅓ cup butter
½ lb. finely chopped fresh mushrooms
2 tbsp. parsley, chopped
¼ tsp. basil
1½ cups fresh breadcrumbs
1 tsp. salt
½ teaspoon pepper
2 tbsp. lemon juice
1 cup dry white wine or water

Preheat oven to 350°F. Dry fish well inside and out with paper towels.

Peel, seed and chop the tomatoes.

Melt ½ the butter in a frying pan, add the onions and stir, over medium heat until limp, but not browned. Add the mushrooms and stir 2 minutes over high heat. Add the chopped tomatoes and simmer 5 minutes. Add the parsley, breadcrumbs, basil, salt and pepper. Mix thoroughly. Stuff fish with mixture. Sew closed or tie with a metal pin.

Place fish in a greased shallow baking pan and sprinkle with the lemon juice and wine. Dot with remaining butter. Bake according to thickness, basting occasionally with the pan juices. It should take from 30 to 40 minutes. Serve hot, garnished with lemon wedges and sprinkled with chopped chives. With this method of cooking, the fish will brown on top and poach underneath. Serves 6.

SAUCES

TARTAR SAUCE

This sauce is the classic accompaniment to fried and baked fish, but it's also good with things like fried mushrooms.

1 cup mayonnaise
2 tbsp. finely chopped sour pickles
1 tbsp. capers
1 small onion, finely chopped
3 sprigs parsley, chopped

Mix ingredients and chill at least 3 hours. Very nice served in a cup of crisped lettuce leaves. Yield: 1 cup.

EGG AND LEMON SAUCE

A perfect sauce for any type of fish, the Greeks know this as *avgolemono*.

3 whole eggs
1 cup lukewarm water or fish stock

1 tbsp. cornstarch
juice of 1 lemon

Beat the eggs until they're well blended and frothy. Add liquid, and cornstarch mixed with lemon juice. Beat well, then stir constantly over low heat until mixture is slightly thickened and smooth (don't boil it). Yield: 1 cup.

LEFTOVER FISH

ENGLISH FISH SALAD

This salad is so good that whenever I cook fish I usually do more than I need so I can make it. Any poached, fried or steamed fish will do, but fried cod, haddock and halibut are the best.

½ lb. cooked fish
3 - 4 cooked potatoes, thinly sliced
1 medium onion, thinly sliced
2 tomatoes, peeled and sliced
2 tbsp. salad oil
1 tbsp. cider or wine vinegar
1 tbsp. strong prepared mustard
½ tsp. salt
¼ tsp. each pepper and turmeric

Break fish into pieces, removing any skin. In a salad bowl make alternate layers of fish, potatoes, onion and tomatoes. Beat remaining ingredients with a rotatry beater and pour over salad. If you wish, surround with a border of finely chopped parsley or chives. Cover and refrigerate 3 - 5 hours before serving. Serves 2 - 3.

FISH SOUFFLE

This is a French chef's recipe and no one can tell it is made with leftover fish. You can use any fish, even cod, but try it some time with leftover fresh salmon.

1 cup cooked or canned fish, shredded
3 tbsp. raw carrots, finely shredded
1 tbsp. parsley, minced
3 tbsp. butter
3 tbsp. flour
1 tsp. salt
1 cup milk
3 egg yolks, beaten
1 tsp. lemon juice
3 egg whites, beaten stiff
butter
lemon juice

Stir together the fish, carrots and parsley. Make a white sauce with the butter, flour, salt and milk, stirring constantly until it is creamy and smooth.

Preheat the oven to 350°F.

Remove the white sauce from the heat and add the fish mixture, stirring until thoroughly blended. Beat the egg yolks until light and beat into the sauce. Add the lemon juice, then fold in the beaten egg whites.

Pour into an unbuttered 1½ quart soufflé or baking dish and set in a pan containing 1 inch of hot water.

85

Bake for 45 minutes, or until well puffed and golden brown.

Serve without delay with a hot lemon butter sauce, made by heating together equal quantities of butter and lemon juice.

MOUSSE MOUSSELINE

Even though made with leftovers, this delicate mousse makes an attractive and tasty buffet or luncheon dish.

2 cups cooked fish fillets
1 envelope unflavored gelatine
1 cup boiling water or clam juice
2 tablespoons fresh lemon juice
¼ tsp. salt
½ cup mayonnaise
1 tsp. Dijon mustard
2 green onions, finely chopped
½ cup chopped celery
½ cup heavy cream, whipped

Flake the fish and set aside. Pour gelatine over ½ cup of cold water, let stand 5 minutes, then dissolve in the boiling water or clam juice. Let cool, add lemon juice, salt, and refrigerate until it has the consistency of unbeaten egg whites.

Mix mayonnaise with mustard, green onions and celery, add flaked fish and combine with gelatine mixture. Fold in whipped cream.

Pour into an oiled 1½ quart mold and refrigerate until firm (it may take up to 6 hours). Unmold onto shredded lettuce. Serves 6.

TUNA

Would you believe that canned tuna is as tasty and good as fresh tuna — something seems to happen to the fish during the processing period which gives it flavor and a good texture.

Fresh tuna is somewhat expensive, not too easy to find on the market, and difficult to cook as only a few seconds too many of broiling or poaching will make it dry.

A few cans of tuna should be kept on the emergency shelf at all times as so many good things can be prepared with it at a few moments' notice.

There are four kinds of fish canned as tuna.

Albacore The very best — it has choice ivory white meat that breaks up in beautiful curved flakes. The albacore is a baby-sized tuna, which runs from 5 to 20 pounds. It is usually packed as a solid pack and being of the very finest quality, it is also the highest priced. Use it for elegant salads or where it stands on its own. You will see the name Albacore on the can.

Skipjack Also a light meat tuna — more plentiful than

the albacore and a bit darker and even smaller, it runs from 5 to 15 pounds.

Yellowfin A bigger tuna — it runs from 100 to 150 pounds and the bigger the yellowfin, the coarser the texture, usually the 100-pound type is used for canning. It is also a light meat tuna.

Bluefin The biggest of them all. I was told by Nova Scotia fishermen that it takes a team of three or four sturdy men to land it. They say that on their coast it sometimes runs up to 1,500 pounds. Of course, the meat is darker and coarser than that of the smaller tuna but it is equally nutritious and flavorsome.

A few fish of the mackerel family, much like tuna, the bonito and the yellowtail, are also canned, but they must display their own names and not be labelled tuna. That explains the difference in texture and flavor between Bonito and Albacore.

All canned tuna is packed in 7-ounce solid pack and 6½-ounce chunk style or flaked.

If you simply turn the tuna out from the can to serve as is with a green salad or a cucumber sauce, which is a very nice lunch and easy to prepare, use the Albacore. To make a casserole or any other dishes, use the one that fits your budget best. The chunks are broken pieces; and the flaked or grated tuna consists of the scraps from packing the other big pieces, it is just as good, but less attractive to look at. When mixed with other food, it matters little.

Tuna is usually packed with salad oil and a small quantity of salt, some packers add vegetable broth. This is important to know as it shows that the juices should not be thrown away, they are also rich in food nutrients. Use them in the preparation of the dishes with tuna.

NOODLE TUNA CUSTARD

Use a 6½-ounce can of flaked or bonito tuna for this casserole, which can be served any day of the year as a family dish and is made in "one-two-three" and in the oven.

¼ cup margarine or bacon fat
½ cup diced celery or 1 green pepper, diced
1 small onion, chopped
1½ cups milk
¼ cup chopped pimiento (optional)
½ lb. milk cheese, cubed
3 eggs, well beaten
½ tsp. salt
4 oz. noodles, cooked
2 cans flaked or bonito tuna

Place in saucepan the margarine or bacon fat, celery or green pepper, onion, milk, pimiento and cheese. Stir occasionally over low heat, until hot and cheese is melted.

Add the eggs and salt, beating well as they are added.

Cook the noodles, drain and mix with the cheese sauce and undrained flaked tuna. Place the mixture in a buttered casserole, set it in a pan of hot water and bake at 350°F., 35 to 40 minutes. Serves 8.

Note: I sometimes use only 1 can of tuna when I want a lighter meal.

TUNA CHINESE STYLE

This is always a nice meal, and it's so very easy to prepare. Serve with fluffy boiled rice and a bottle of soya sauce.

3 tbsp. salad oil
1 onion, thinly sliced
3 celery stalks, bias sliced
1 small green pepper, in long slivers
½ tsp. sugar
¼ tsp. monosodium glutamate
1 large can flaked tuna
2 tbsp. cornstarch
2 tbsp. soya sauce
⅛ tsp. garlic powder
¼ cup water

Heat the oil in a large frying pan, add the onion, celery and green pepper, stir constantly over high heat for 1 minute. Add the sugar and msg., stir a few seconds. Add the flaked tuna, blend in for 1 minute.

Mix the cornstarch with the soya sauce, garlic powder and water. Pour over the mixture and stir a few seconds. Cover and cook over low heat 2 - 3 minutes and serve immediately. The vegetables will be cooked, but slightly crisp, as is usual with Chinese food. Serves 6.

CHINESE SWEET AND SOUR TUNA

Another quick delight for those who like Chinese Sweet and Sour food. Albacore or other types can be used, the flavor will be just as good, but the appearance of the dish is better with Albacore tuna.

6 slices canned pineapple
2 tbsp. butter
⅔ cup of the pineapple syrup or
⅔ cup pineapple juice
2 green peppers
2 tbsp. cornstarch
2 tsp. soy sauce
2 tbsp. cider vinegar
2 tbsp. sugar
1 cup chicken bouillon or consommé
2 cans tuna
½ tsp. salt
¼ tsp. pepper

Drain pineapple and cut each slice into sixths. Sauté in the butter over high heat for about 5 minutes. Add ⅓ cup of the pineapple juice (the juice is better than the syrup because it has more piquancy) and the green pepper.

Mix the cornstarch with the remaining ⅓ cup of pineapple juice. Add to pineapple mixture with the soy sauce, vinegar, sugar and bouillon or consommé. Cook over medium heat, stirring constantly, until thick and creamy. Add the tuna, undrained, salt and pepper. Heat thoroughly. Serve with boiled rice. Serves 6.

TUNA LUNCHEON SALAD

One of the nicest salads, I learned to make it from

one of the top French chefs, Chef Mondage of Chailly-en-Bière, near the Forest of Fontainebleau, where my husband used to go riding. Its distinction is the seasoning of the salad, a plain dressing and a topping of Mayonnase Anglaise, as he used to call it, which is simply an excellent boiled dressing.

1 7-oz. can Albacore tuna
1¼ cups fine diced celery
½ cup cooked green peas
½ cup cooked diced carrots
3 tbsp. salad oil
1 tbsp. cider vinegar
¼ tsp. dry mustard
a pinch curry powder
½ tsp. salt
pinch of sugar

Place the tuna in a bowl and break into large flakes. Add the celery, green peas and carrots. The quantity and type of vegetables can be varied to suit your taste and need; fresh cooked or canned vegetables can be used. Then add the salad oil, vinegar, dry mustard, curry powder, salt and sugar. Toss lightly together. Refrigerate dressing.

Measure 2½ tablespoons of butter in the top of a double boiler. Stir in ½ teaspoon dry mustard, ½ teaspoon salt, 2 teaspoons sugar and 2 teaspoons cornstarch. Beat and add 1 egg. Mix well and stir in ¾ cup light cream. Cook and stir over hot water until the mixture gets creamy and all the starchy feeling is gone. It should have the consistency of heavy thick cream. Refrigerate until cold.

To serve the salad, heap portions in cups of lettuce. Top with a teaspoon of cooked dressing. Put the rest in a bowl to serve with the salad. Serves 4 to 6.

TUNA FISH FLORENTINE

The classic recipe of this gourmet dish is prepared with fresh poached fillets of sole, set on a bed of spinach, topped a special sauce and cheese. It is much quicker and less costly to prepare with tuna and just as elegant.

1 lb. fresh spinach
1 tbsp. flour
1 tsp. butter
4 tbsp. butter
4 tbsp. flour
2 cups milk
½ tsp. salt
½ cup grated Parmesan cheese
2 egg yolks, lightly beaten
¼ tsp. pepper
2 6½-oz. cans tuna

Wash the spinach and place in a large saucepan without any water. Cover and cook over medium heat for 2 minutes, turn the spinach, cover and cook another 2 minutes. Pour into a sieve and drain excess water. Put the spinach back in the pan. Sprinkle top with the tablespoon of flour, add the teaspoon of butter, and stir together over low heat, until the spinach is creamy. Salt and pepper to taste. Spread in a shallow well buttered, baking dish.

Make a white sauce with the 4 tablespoons butter, flour and the milk. When smooth and creamy, add the salt and Parmesan cheese. Stir until well mixed. Remove from the heat and add the beaten eggs and pepper, stirring all the time. Taste for seasoning. Measure ½ cup of the sauce and pour over the spinach. Top with the flaked tuna. Pour the remaining sauce on top of the tuna. Sprinkle the top, to taste, with an additional tablespoon of Parmesan cheese.

Heat in a 375°F. oven until the sauce bubbles around the edges, about 15 minutes.

To glaze the top, run under the broiler for a few seconds. Tuna Florentine can be prepared ahead of time, except for the cooking, and kept refrigerated until ready to use. The cooking period may then require a few minutes more. Serves 6.

SARDINES

Basically, a sardine is a small pilchard canned in oil, but there are many, many types of these canned fish and they differ widely.

The fish caught in the cool, mineral-rich waters of Norwegian fjords have a quality of their own because they can be kept alive in nets until almost the very moment the packing process begins. They are lightly smoked over slow burning oak fires that give them a special flavor and color.

French and Portuguese sardines are quite different; they're unsmoked and they are plumper, bigger, and more meaty. To discover which you prefer, you must read the label carefully to see what type of fish the can contains, how it is packed and what country it comes from.

The most common varieties are the brisling and the sild. Brisling are characterized by their juicy plumpness, while sild have firmer flesh.

Since sardines lend themselves to such a countless variety of dishes, for every meal of the day, I think we should learn to do a little more than merely open the can.

SAVO BREAKFAST

These scrambled eggs are at home any time — breakfast, luncheon or late snack. They are particularly good when served with smoked Norwegian sardines.

4 slices rye bread, toasted
4 - 6 eggs, scrambled
1 can sardines, well drained
parsley, chopped
radishes, sliced
celery sticks

Butter the toasted bread and set each piece on its own warm plate. Top with soft, creamy scrambled eggs. Place 3 - 5 sardines on top of the eggs and sprinkle generously with parsley.

Serve with sliced radishes, celery sticks and ketchup in separate dishes and let each person help himself. Serves 4.

SARDINE SALAD PARISIENNE

This colorful, tasty dish can be served at luncheon or as a first course for dinner. I also like it for picnics. It is very attractive when a long, narrow dish is used.

½ cup cooked carrots, diced
1 cup cooked potatoes, diced
1 cup frozen green peas
3 tbsp. mayonnaise
2 tbsp. cream or top milk
1 green onion, finely chopped

peel of 1 orange, grated
2 hard boiled eggs
1 can sardines

Cool the carrots and potatoes and place in separate bowls. Cook green peas according to directions on package, but drain and let cold water run on them until they are completely cooled. This will keep them firm and a bright green color. Drain thoroughly and place in a bowl.

Blend the mayonnaise with the cream or top milk, green onion, and grated orange peel. Mix each vegetable with some of the mayonnaise. Taste for seasoning. Set on a long dish in a row, placing the green peas in the middle. Slice the eggs, arrange slices on top of the vegetables. Top each egg slice with a sardine and sprinkle each sardine with a bit of chopped parsley. Garnish with lemon wedges and parsley. Serves 4 - 6.

SCALLOPED SARDINES

The Scandinavian countries have long known the pleasure of eating golden scalloped potatoes with sardines. It is a gourmet dish at low cost.

3 - 4 medium potatoes, peeled
2 medium onions, thinly sliced
2 cans sardines, well-drained
3 eggs
½ tsp. turmeric
pinch of nutmeg
1½ cups milk
4 tbsp. butter, melted

Grease a 1½ quart casserole with butter. Cover bottom with a layer of thinly sliced, raw potatoes; brush with a bit of melted butter. Place a layer of onions on top, then a layer of sardines. Salt and pepper lightly.

Repeat layers, but change the order so that the next layer will be onion, the next sardines and the top layer potatoes.

Beat the eggs with the turmeric and nutmeg. Add milk and melted butter, salt and pepper to taste. Pour over potatoes and bake at 350°F. for 50 - 60 minutes, or until the potatoes are tender and golden. Serves 4 - 6.

BAKED SARDINES FLORENTINE

In Genoa and Venice, this dish is made with fresh sardines. I was curious to try this favorite made with fresh fish, but it was not as good as it is with canned sardines.

> 1 tbsp. butter
> 1½ tbsp. flour
> ¾ cup milk
> pinch of nutmeg
> 2 tbsp. cheese, diced
> 1 bag of spinach
> 1 can sardines, well drained
> 2 hard boiled eggs, sliced
> 3 boiled potatoes, thinly sliced

Melt butter in frying pan, add the flour and stir well. Add the milk, stir until creamy and smooth. Add the nutmeg, diced cheese, and salt and pepper to taste. Stir over very low heat until the cheese is melted.

To cook the spinach, pour contents of cello bag into a bowl of cold water. Rinse well and lift to a large saucepan. Place covered over medium heat, cook 5 minutes, turning over once. Drain in a sieve, put back in saucepan and salt and pepper to taste. Cut up with a good-sized piece of butter.

Place half the cheese sauce in a shallow baking dish. Top with the spinach, then with the sardines. On one side of the sardines, place the hard boiled eggs and on the other, the potatoes. Pour the remaining sauce entirely over. Sprinkle with a bit of paprika and bake at 400°F. for 10 minutes. Serves 4.

OSKA DAVIDSEN SARDINE OPEN FACE

The world-renowned Danish sandwich maker and cold table expert has quite a way with sardines. The following are from the famous 4-foot long Smorgasbord menu in his restaurants, and they are ideal for TV snacks or a summer garden meal.

Have ready thinly sliced dark and light rye bread, assorted large crackers and soft butter, preferably unsalted. Place the following garnishes on generously buttered bread and complete the cold table with dishes of radishes, celery, olives and pickles.

— Sardines (5 or 6) topped with curry mayonnaise (a little curry powder beaten into mayonnaise).
— Sardines sprinkled with lemon juice, topped with dill mayonnaise (add fresh or dried dill to mayonnaise).
— Thinly sliced mushrooms topped with a layer of scrambled eggs, then with a row of sardines.

- Small smoked sardines covered completely with thinly sliced cucumbers.
- Finely diced potato salad topped with thinly sliced pickled beets and sardines.
- Sardines, one half sprinkled with grated hard boiled eggs, the other with finely minced parsley or chives.
- Chutney spread and topped with sardines and 2 half slices of cooked bacon.

FRESH HERRING, MARINATED

Any type of small fresh herring will do, or use thawed frozen smelt.

1½ lbs. small fresh herring
2 tbsp. cider vinegar
6 tbsp. salad oil
1 tsp. sugar
2 tbsp. tomato paste
1 tsp. salt
½ tsp. pepper

Clean the herring, or ask the fish dealer to do it. Wash thoroughly in cold, salted water and drain on absorbent paper. Place them side by side in a baking dish (do not use a metal one). Stir together the rest of the ingredients and pour over the fish. Cover with a lid or foil paper and simmer over low heat for 10 minutes. Cool and refrigerate for 24 hours before serving.

These are very good with a bowl of unseasoned greens and a plate of cucumber sticks. Let each person use some of the fish liquid as a salad dressing. Serves 4.

SMOKED FISH RÖKET

A delicious Norwegian specialty, this can be prepared and served in 15 minutes. Enjoy it with French bread, toasted and buttered, and cucumber slices.

½ to ¾ lb. smoked fish
freshly ground black pepper, to taste
¼ cup heavy cream
3 tbsp. fine dry breadcrumbs
1 tsp. butter

Generously butter a small, shallow baking dish and place the fish in it. Sprinkle with pepper, pour cream over, then sprinkle with breadcrumbs and dot with butter.

Bake uncovered in a preheated 400°F. oven about 10 minutes, or until the fish is hot. Serves 1 or 2.

SHRIMP

BUTTERFLY SHRIMP

Through the years, I have been asked for this recipe
more often than any other. Not only shrimp but squares
of halibut or pieces of lobster can be prepared in this
way. Of course, they will not be "butterfly" but the suc-
culent taste will be the same.

1 lb. raw shrimp, shelled
1 tbsp, soy sauce
1 tsp. sherry
½ tsp. salt
¼ tsp. monosodium glutamate
thick slice fresh ginger, peeled and grated
2 eggs, beaten
1½ tbsp. cornstarch
1½ tbsp. flour
corn or peanut oil for frying

Cut shelled shrimp halfway through on inner curve

and spread out to form a butterfly. The cutting is done with scissors or a sharp knife.

Mix together the soy sauce, sherry, salt, monosodium glutamate and grated ginger. Roll shrimp in this mixture and marinate for 15 minutes to an hour. Remove from mixture and dry thoroughly with absorbent paper. Mix the eggs, constarch and flour and dip each shrimp in this mixture until well coated. Fry the shrimp in 2 inches of hot oil until they are golden, and serve while hot. Serves 4.

SHRIMP VOLLARTA

Simple and most elegant.

> 1½ lbs. fresh jumbo shrimp
> juice of 1 or 2 fresh limes
> 2 tsp. coarse kosher salt
> 2 to 3 tbsp. mild salad oil

Split the fresh shrimp in half lengthwise through the shell and tail. Rinse out dark vein. Dry shrimp on paper towels, place in flat dish and sprinkle cut side generously with the lime juice. Sprinkle with salt. Let stand in refrigerator a couple of hours, if possible.

At serving time, heat salad oil in a large heavy frying pan. Add about half the shrimp at a time; sauté until the shells are pink, no more than 2 or 3 minutes on each side. Heap onto a warm platter with lots of quartered fresh limes. Serve shrimp as a hot appetizer for 6, or as a supper entrée for 3. Pass small plates with appetizer and plenty of paper napkins. Or another thoughtful gesture — pass a tray of finger tip towels, dipped in hot water, wrung dry and rolled tightly.

POTTED SHRIMP

There are many ways of making this well known English specialty, but the very best I've ever tasted are those at the world famous Ivy restaurant in London; it is a paste of shrimp made with whole shrimp.

1 cup unsalted butter
1 garlic clove, crushed
1 lb. small cooked shrimp or
4 cans cocktail shrimp, 3 oz. each
¼ tsp. tarragon or thyme
¾ tsp. salt
¼ tsp. pepper
⅛ tsp. mace

Melt ¾ cup of the butter, add garlic and half of shrimp. Heat thoroughly over very low heat, but briefly and don't simmer. Add seasonings and purée by blending covered, or passing through a sieve, or mashing with a fork; whatever method is used, the mixture must be creamy.

Heat the rest of shrimp in the remaining ¼ cup of butter and add to the puréed mixture. Stir gently until mixture starts to cool — it's quicker if the bowl is set over ice cubes.

Pack mixture into crocks or little dishes and over with foil or plastic wrap. Refrigerate until ready to serve; it will keep 3 - 4 days. While good served with melba toast or thinly sliced and buttered brown bread, at the Ivy it is spread on a thin slice of smoked salmon and sprinkled with pepper. Yield: 6 small crocks.

LOBSTER

POACHED LOBSTER TAILS

For a deluxe cold fish platter and a special party, these should always be included. But don't worry, a fish platter with only one seafood is still very acceptable.

4 frozen lobster tails, thawed
1 cup each dry white wine and boiling water
1½ tsp. salt

The lobster tails should total about 2¼ lbs. You can add one or two more if you wish. Split each lengthwise with a sharp knife or scissors and, if large enough, in half again to make 4 pieces. Bring to a boil with remaining ingredients, then immediately cover and remove from heat. Let stand 20 minutes, or until shells turn pink.

Drain tails from liquid, let cool and leave at room temperature until needed . Some may prefer to remove the shells, but in the true Scandinavian manner, the cooked pieces remain in their shells.

111

LOBSTER CARDINAL

Using fresh, frozen or even canned lobster, this dish will be spectacular and delicious. Part of the work is done early in the morning; the last touches take only a few minutes to do in your chafing dish.

2 tbsp. flour
¾ cup light cream
1 tsp. curry powder
½ tsp. turmeric
salt and pepper, to taste
4 tbsp. brandy or whisky
⅔ cup tomato sauce
¼ tsp. tarragon
½ tsp. sugar
3 tbsp. butter
1 - 1½ lbs. lobster meat
1 cup long grain rice

In the morning, blend the flour with the cream until smooth, then cook over low heat, stirring all the time, until creamy. Add the curry powder, turmeric, salt and pepper.

Beat with a whisk or a hand beater until the sauce is well blended. Pour into an attractive container. Cover with a piece of wax paper, with the paper touching the sauce to prevent a crust forming.

On a tray, place the container of cream sauce and, in small bowls, the brandy or whisky, and the tomato sauce stirred with the tarragon and sugar. Add a wooden spoon to cook with, and a medium-sized serving spoon. Get your chafing dish (or any other utensil you wish to cook with) ready to be taken out. Keep the butter and lobster refrigerated until you are ready to start cooking.

To make the rice ahead of time: boil it according to the package directions. Drain, then rinse under running cold water. Pour into a baking dish that has a cover. Place dots of butter on top of the rice. Salt and pepper lightly and cover. About 5 minutes before serving, place the dish over low heat, covered. After 5 minutes, stir with a fork. It will be hot and ready to serve.

To finish the Lobster Cardinal, melt the butter in a chafing dish over a good flame, or in an electric frying pan at 350°. Add the lobster, and stir for a few minutes to warm it up. Pour the brandy or whisky on top and warm up for 2 - 4 seconds. Set a match to it and blaze. Add the cooked cream sauce and the tomato sauce mixture. Stir gently until the whole is well mixed and hot.

This is very nice served *à la Chinoise* in small individual bowls. The rice can be served in one large bowl, or in a separate bowl for each guest. Serves 4.

LOBSTER QUICHE

Crab can replace the lobster and still make as tasty a quiche. For a large party, it is nice to make individual quiches.

pastry of your choice
2 cups lobster meat
1 cup white wine or chicken broth
½ lb. fresh mushrooms, thinly sliced
¼ lb. Swiss cheese, thinly sliced

113

3 eggs
1 tbsp. all purpose flour
pinch each of nutmeg, curry powder
½ tsp. salt
½ cup light cream

Line a 9 inches pie plate or 8 tart shells with pastry. Use canned, thawed frozen, or boiled fresh lobster and cut it into bite-sized pieces. Heat wine or chicken broth with mushrooms about 10 minutes over low heat, then drain, reserving liquid.

Place lobster and drained mushrooms in alternate layers in a pie shell, with sliced cheese between each layer.

Lightly beat eggs with remaining ingredients and ½ cup of the reserved lquid. Pour over pie contents and bake at 375°F. for 25 - 35 minutes, or until golden brown and the custard is set. Serves 8.

If making a day or two early, refrigerate, then warm at 300°F. for 15 minutes. Or just let it return to room temperature.

CANTONESE LOBSTER

This Chinese method of cooking makes a faster feast than any other. One or two 5-oz. cans of lobster can be used instead of the frozen; even with this rather small amount there will be enough to serve four generously.

1 lb. frozen rock lobster tails
1 cup long grain rice
2 tbsp. cornstarch
¼ cup peanut or sesame oil

114

soy sauce
2 cloves garlic, peeled and minced
¼ lb. (½ cup) ground pork
1 tsp. salt
¼ tsp. each pepper and ground ginger
½ tsp. sugar
6 green onions, thinly sliced
1 cup celery, thinly sliced on the bias
1 cup spinach or lettuce, coarsely cut
1 cup mayonnaise

If using the rock lobster tails, thaw in refrigerator section during the day. Remove meat from shells and slice ¼ - ½ inch thick.

Measure and prepare all the ingredients to be used. Put rice on to cook. Mix the cornstarch with 3 tbsp. of water. Heat plates or serving dish.

Set a large frying pan or a Chinese wok over high heat and add the oil. When hot, add 2 teaspoons of soy sauce and the garlic. Stir constantly until garlic begins to brown. Add pork and stir for 1 minute, then remove with a slotted spoon to a warm plate.

Stir into frying pan 1 tablespoon of soy sauce, the seasonings, green onions, celery, and spinach or lettuce. Mix and toss until well coated with fat.

Add lobster and stir about 1 minute. Return pork to mixture. Add consommé, cornstarch and stir quickly, still over high heat until thickened and clear. Arrange over rice. Serves 4.

SCALLOPS

COQUILLES ST. JACQUES

Many travellers to France have enjoyed these creamed scallops served in their shells. This classic dish can be prepared ahead of time and baked when you're ready.

2 lbs. scallops
2 cups any white wine
1 bay leaf
¼ tsp. thyme
1 celery leaf
3 sprigs parsley
1 tsp. salt
6 tbsp. butter
½ cup chopped mushrooms
6 green onions, chopped
1 tbsp. finely chopped parsley
1 tsp. bottled lemon juice
¼ cup water
3 egg yolks

½ cup cream
4 tbsp. flour
½ cup fine dry breadcrumbs
4 tbsp. grated Parmesan

If frozen, thaw the scallops just enough to separate. Simmer next 6 ingredients 5 minutes, add scallops and simmer 8 minutes. Drain, reserving broth, and chop scallops coarsely.

Melt 2 tablespoons of the butter in a saucepan, add mushrooms, onions, parsley, lemon juice and water. Mix well, cover and simmer 10 minutes over medium heat. Strain, reserving vegetables, and add liquid to wine broth. Beat egg yolks with the cream.

Melt remaining 4 tablespoons of butter in a saucepan, add flour and mix well. Add combined liquids and cook over medium heat, stirring constantly, 3 - 4 minutes or until creamy and smooth. Remove from heat and stir in egg yolk mixture with a whisk or wooden spoon. Taste for seasoning and stir in scallops, green onions and mushrooms.

Heap this thick mixture into scallop shells or individual dishes and sprinkle with breadcrumbs mixed with cheese. Bake in a 450°F. oven 5 - 8 minutes, or until brown on top. Serves 6 - 8.

WEST COAST SCALLOPS

This delectable way of serving scallops requires the bare minimum of cooking.

1 lb. scallops
1 tbsp. lemon juice
1 cup water or white wine
2 grapefruit
¼ cup melted butter
salt and paprika, to taste
watercress or parsley

If frozen, thaw the scallops just enough to separate them. Bring to a boil over high heat with lemon juice and water or wine, then cover and simmer over very low heat 5 - 6 minutes. Drain and cut scallops across into ¼-inch slices.

Peel the grapefruit, leaving no white skin, and cut into sections, discarding membrane. Arrange sections with scallops in 6 generously buttered scallop shells, or individual oven proof ramekins, or a shallow baking dish.

Pour melted butter over evenly and sprinkle lightly with salt and paprika. Bake in a 350°F. oven 6 minutes, or until heated through, then sprinkle generously with chopped watercress or parsley and garnish with sprigs of either. Serves 6.

BAKED SCALLOPS

Cooking them in the oven at a high temperature ensures crispness, uses less fat, takes less attention, and eliminates frying odors.

1 lb. scallops
1 cup milk
½ tsp. salt

½ tsp. turmeric (optional)
1½ cups fine dry breadcrumbs
1 tsp. paprika
¼ cup melted butter or oil

If frozen, thaw and dry the scallops. Dip into a mixture of the milk, salt and turmeric, then into breadcrumbs mixed with paprika. Place in a well greased baking dish, and brush each with melted butter or oil. Bake in a 500°F. oven (make sure it has reached that temperature) for no more than 8 minutes and serve immediately, with Remoulade Sauce (see next recipe) or plain mayonnaise. Serves 6.

SAUTEED SCALLOP REMOULADE

The Remoulade sauce, similar to but more delicate than tartar is the best choice with sautéed or pan-fried scallops, be they breaded or plain.

1 lb. scallops
1 tsp. salt
¼ tsp. pepper
2 eggs
2 tbsp. milk
1 cup fine bread or cracker crumbs
salad oil
Remoulade Sauce (see below)

If frozen, thaw and dry the scallops, then sprinkle with the salt and pepper. Dip each into eggs beaten with milk, then roll in crumbs and let dry 15 - 20 minutes, uncovered, on a platter.

Heat ¼-inch of salad oil in a cast iron frying pan, but don't let it smoke. Fry scallops over moderate heat, 3 minutes per side, or until golden brown. Set on a warm platter and serve the following sauce separately. Serves 6.

Remoulade Sauce: Combine 1 cup of mayonnaise, 2 teaspoons of prepared French mustard, 2 small minced gherkins, 1 tablespoon each of capers and chopped parsley, ½ teaspoon of dried tarragon, 1 small, finely chopped onion, salt and pepper to taste. Yield: 1¼ cups.

SCALLOPS CANTONESE

Here, the brief cooking time and perfect seasoning enhance the delicate flavor of the scallops. Serve with instant canned fried rice for a complete meal.

> 1 lb. scallops
> 1 tbsp. cornstarch
> 4 tbsp. cold water
> 1½ tbsp. salad or sesame oil
> 1½ tsp. salt
> 1 green onion, in small pieces
> 2 slices fresh ginger (optional)

If frozen, thaw and dry the scallops. Cut each across in 4 slices. Mix cornstarch, cold water and set aside.

Heat oil in a large frying pan over high heat, add scallops and stir for 1 minute. Add salt, green onions and ginger (use nothing but fresh) and stir over high heat for 2 minutes. Add cornstarch mixture and stir for 1 minute

121

over low heat, or until pan juices become translucent and creamy (the scallop slices will be opaque). Serve immediately. Serves 4.

LONDON DELIGHT

A few years ago, during a stroll in London, I stopped in front of a beautiful display of fresh fish and shellfish. The fishmonger gave me this amazingly good, but simple idea for scallops, and I now serve it often with toasted Hovis bread.

1 lb. scallops
½ - ¾ lb. side bacon
chutney

Use fresh scallops if possible, but if using frozen, thaw and dry them. Place side by side in bottom of a shallow broiler pan and put bacon on grill rack over them. Cook in a 475°F. oven until the bacon is crisped and browned, about 5 minutes.

Remove grill and bacon, cook scallops another 4 minutes, then place on a warm platter. Salt and pepper to taste, surround with bacon and serve with a bowl of chutney. Serves 4.

CRAB

CRAB QUICHE

I learned to make this while spending a few days with a fisherman's family in Covey Cove. N.S. This is my variation of his wife's lobster pie.

pie crust of your choice, thinly rolled
1 cup mushrooms, sliced
2 tbsp. brandy or lemon juice
1 cup canned crab
¼ lb. Swiss or mild Cheddar cheese, grated
3 eggs
1 tbsp. all purpose flour
⅛ tsp. nutmeg
½ tsp. salt
1 cup cream

Line 8 2-inch aluminum tart pans with the thinly rolled pastry.

Preheat oven to 375°F.

Combine and stir the mushrooms with the brandy or lemon juice, then shred the crab, removing any hard parts. Fill each tart with alternate layers of sliced mushrooms, crab and grated cheese.

Beat together the eggs, flour, nutmeg, salt and cream, then pour equally over each tart. Place in a baking pan and bake for 20 - 30 minutes, or until the custard is set and the top golden brown. Serves 8.

If you are preparing this in advance, cool thoroughly and wrap each tart individually in a square of foil. Refrigerate or freeze. To reheat, unwrap and place in a 375°F. oven for 10 - 15 minutes.

SEAFOOD AVOCADO SALAD

Winter vacationers to Florida or Mexico will remember this salad. It is also easy to have in Canada, even when snow covers the ground.

1 cup or 15-oz. can lobster meat
1 lb. fresh shrimps, cooked
1 cup or 15-oz. can crabmeat
½ cup French dressing
3 avocados
lemon juice
1 tsp. cider or wine vinegar
¼ tsp. tarragon
¼ tsp. salt
¼ tsp. dry mustard
¼ cup mayonnaise
¼ cup sour cream
chives or parsley, minced

Use the safood as listed, or an equal quantity of one of the three, or any mixture to suit your taste. Add the French dressing and toss to coat evenly. Cover and refrigerate at least 4 hours, preferably overnight.

Cut the avocados in half lengthwise and remove the pits. Brush the cut surface with lemon juice and mound the seafood into each half.

Make the topping by stirring together the vinegar, tarragon, salt and mustard. Blend together the mayonnaise and sour cream and fold in the vinegar mixture.

Spoon some of the topping onto each avocado half, sprinkle with chives or parsley and serve with small, hot baking powder biscuits. Serves 6.

FRUIT AND SEAFOOD SALAD

Perfect for a hot evening, this can be an entrée or a main course. Any mayonnaise is suitable, but the sour cream type is well worth the making.

1 head of lettuce
1 lb. fresh, frozen or canned crabmeat (about 2 cups)
15-oz. can sockeye salmon
2 grapefruit
1 avocado and juice of 1 lemon (optional)
approx. 1½ cups mayonnaise
¼ cup minced fresh chives

Wash the lettuce and break off leaves. Place them in ice cold water for 1 hour, drain and refrigerate wrapped in absorbent paper for 1 - 2 days (the longer they sit, the crisper they'll be).

To serve, arrange a bed of crisp lettuce leaves on 6 salad plates. Place a mound of crabmeat and one of flaked salmon in centre of each. Peel grapefruit and cut into sections. Peel avocado and slice into thin slivers, dipping them in lemon juice to prevent discoloration.

Arrange grapefruit and avocado in radiating spokes around the seafood. Top each salad with mayonnaise to taste and sprinkle chives over all. Serves 6.

If you wish to make sour cream mayonnaise for this, beat 2 egg yolks with 1 tablespoon of dry mustard and ½ teaspoon of salt, using an electric mixer. Gradually beat in 1 cup of salad oil, adding if drop by drop until it starts to thicken, then by tablespoonfuls. When all the oil has been added and the mayonnaise is thick, mix in 2 tablespoons of fresh or bottled lemon juice.

Stir in ½ cup of commercial sour cream and keep refrigerated until ready to use — it will keep 3 weeks. Yield: about 1½ cups.